The Forgotten People

By

Vera Reynolds

Vera Reynolds ©

The Forgotten People

© Vera Reynolds

This Book is licensed for your personal enjoyment only. This Book may not be re-sold or given away to other people. If you would like to share this book with another person, please purchase an additional copy for each recipient. If you're reading this book and did not purchase it, or it was not purchased for your use only, then please purchase your own copy. Thank you for respecting the hard work of this author

The Story of The Forgotten People

This is a story about two groups of people separated by time, culture and distance and pushed beyond the limits of human endurance by the people governing their respective countries. Yet, by rights they should have been enemies, but to this day they are linked together because of an unconditional act of love and personal sacrifice born out of understanding from one group of human beings to another in the face of adversity. Greater love hath no man! Because of their wonderful brave and valiant spirit both cultures have survived. Sadly however, vast numbers did not. There aren't any records to show the existence of most of them.

It is for these people that I will endeavour to write and hopefully do justice to this story in honour of their sacred memory.

The Background to the Story

The two periods of history relevant to the story are 1831 – 1833 and 1845 – 1849.

They relate to the Native American Indians and the people of Ireland during the famine and the great similarities in the suffering and fate of Two Peoples, Oceans Apart.

The period, 1831-1833 relates to the removals of the Native American Indians. In this case the Choctaw Indians who lived, by hunting and farming, in the areas of Mississippi, Alabama and Louisiana. They were peaceful people. Over a three year period approximately 40,000 Choctaw in total, were forced to leave their lands and move west to what is now known as the state of Oklahoma. The name was derived from the Choctaw language. Okla Homa, which means "Red People." Only two thirds survived the journey that became known as "The Trails of Tears."

The first removal took place in the autumn of 1831.Their journey was beset by fierce weather conditions. Following floods, a blizzard set in with strong northerly winds bringing snow and sleet swirling across the hills. As well as starvation through lack of supplies; cholera, typhus and dysentery were rampant especially amongst the elders and the very young. The Indians were rounded up and herded from their homes like animals. They had to leave behind everything they owned. Women were stopped in their tracks in the middle of such chores as making bread as men were stopped in their tracks in the same way out in their lands. They had to leave all their belongings behind as well as their land, cattle and anything else of value. They were promised help along the way, food and provisions in plenty and upon arrival at the new lands compensation for the land and cattle left behind. Also they were promised that on arrival they would be given new land. These promises were never fulfilled. Greedy agents in charge of their supplies sold them for personal gain. Along the way some of the military absconded. There were no proper arrangements made for the removals. Most of the Indians were scantily clad and some of the children were near naked because the weather was fine when they were rounded up. They were ushered from their homes in the clothes they stood up in and held in military forts for several weeks where the women were treated with little or no respect, by their captors. The onset of fierce weather and floods was the climate in which they started that first never to be forgotten five hundred mile journey west. The weather worsened along the way and blizzards set in. The Choctaws died by the thousand and very often because the ground was frozen, making burial impossible, the corpses were piled high and burned. Many had the telltale green stains around their mouths from eating grass trying to survive. There are no records of these deaths. A Choctaw Chief described the journey as "A Trail of Tears and Death." A newspaper picked up on the quotation of "The Trails of Tears," and it was later used to describe other Indian removals especially the Cherokee removal in the year 1838 which, apparently defied description.

The period, 1845 –1849 relates to the Potato Famine in Ireland.

The year 1847 was known as "Black 47" the year of mass emigration and death as a result of the potato crop failure of 1845 and 1846. However, 1849, the year Queen Victoria visited Ireland, was the worst year of the famine. In the autumn of 1848 came the devastating blow that the potato crop had failed yet again. Evictions were on the increase and yet in a country reeling from four years of famine, in a single day in November 1848 the list of food exported from Cork to England read as follows;

147 Bales of bacon

120 casks and 135 barrels of pork

5 Casks of hams

149 Casks miscellaneous provisions

1,996 Sacks and 950 barrels of oats

300 Bags of flour

300 Head of cattle

239 Sheep

9,398 Firkins of butter

542 Boxes of eggs.

During the famine Ireland lost at least 3 million people to death and emigration. But like the Choctaws Trails of Tears the mass exodus from Ireland, in what became known as the coffin ships where living conditions defied description and typhus, cholera, dysentery and relapsing fever were rampant, could be called "Voyages of Tears and Death." People died by the thousand. There are no accurate accounts of the numbers buried at sea but it is commonly accepted that from Ireland to Grosse Isle, the quarantine station for Canada, in the ocean graveyard, bodies could form a continuous chain of burial crosses. James Joyce once described the Atlantic as "A Bowl of Sand Filled with Tears," others described it as "The Biggest Graveyard in the World."

In March 1847 the Chief of the Choctaw Indians heard about the plight of the people of Ireland. So moved was he by the story that he called a meeting of the elders.

Having discussed and indeed debated the situation it was generally agreed that it was their duty to help their brothers who were starving in this place called Ireland. Through many personal sacrifices a collection was made and the sum of $170 was raised. This generous gesture was all the more amazing when it should be considered that the Choctaws were forced to leave their lands because of the arrival of the Europeans. They brought with them illnesses that were responsible for thousands of deaths amongst the Indian tribes who had no immunity against the white man's diseases. To this day the two nations are closely connected by an organisation called Celts and American Indians Together. CAIT, as it is known, aims to raise $1.7 million for world famine relief in order to complete the circle of giving started in 1847. In May 1990 a group of Choctaws, including a former chief, took part in a 12-mile walk, following the route where the famine victims perished in Co. Mayo. They called it "The Trail of Tears." A red oak tree was planted in a nearby Anglican Church to commemorate the occasion.

The Core of the Story

County Mayo in the west of Ireland was one of the most densely populated counties during the famine years. Nine tenths of the people depended on the potato for survival.

In the middle of the winter of 1849, in a small town in that county, several hundred starving people from the surrounding hinterlands gathered to seek food and some needed shelter. Because there wasn't any help there for them to be had they were advised to go and put their request to the local landlord who lived about twelve miles across the hills. Men, women and children, the old and the young, sick sore and sorry set out across the hills on a cold grey dawn, most of them scantily clad and barefoot. Women with only a shawl to protect them and the babies that snuggled to their bosoms against the bitter forces of nature in that bleak and barren land of no hope. After a most hazardous journey they arrived at the landlords residence at lunchtime; there was no lunch for this bedraggled starving band of people.   They were left standing around in the rain for some considerable time whilst the landlord entertained his guests to luncheon. Eventually, the landlord's agent came out and told them to "clear off back home, there's nothing here for ye."

Imagine the mutterings and mumblings that must have swept through the crowd. Nothing here for them indeed and himself within in the house with his roast dinner and fine wines no doubt. Angry skirmishes would have ensued especially as the men, who had to listen to the children's cries from cold and hunger, were helpless to do anything about it. People already skeletal in appearance with dark circles around sunken eyes, protruding cheekbones and unsmiling lips hiding randomly spaced teeth, if any, most likely decayed from lack of nourishment because of the ravages of famine that had swept their land for the past four years. Many of these people would have been victims of evictions whereby they would have had had to witness the "tumblings" of their beloved little cottages and not been given time to collect personal belongings as they were forced out onto the open countryside by the landlords agent and his henchmen. Parents could not take in children or vice versa because if they did then they in turn would have had their homes tumbled. Many a heart breaking farewell took place amidst the anguished cries of old folk who witnessed their homes being tumbled. Sons or daughters would have to stand by powerless to help and watch their parents wander down the road, often carrying a sick grandfather or grandmother, to certain death or the workhouse. To them going to the workhouse was like going to hell.

Therefore, it was with heads bowed against the rain and an overwhelming sense of defeat that the famine walkers set off on their homeward path. Heartsick because of the hopelessness of their situation they resigned themselves to whatever fate had in store. The weather worsened. A blizzard set in. A small river at full flood that snaked its way in and out through the bleak and barren hills had to be crossed three times. A large number, probably most of them were lost in the first crossing. Trudging through deep snow and battling fierce winds the rest died across the hills. Not one of them made it back home. In my story a priest, Fr. Patrick Joseph O'Malley, will have survived and through him the story will have been passed down through the ages. It is very likely that the priest might well have accompanied them anyway. Today's telling of the story will also have a Fr. Patrick Joseph O'Malley, a descendant of course, known as Fr. Pat. If this were a film the one actor would play both parts and there would be a happy ending.

In reality this part of the story would start with evictions and "tumblings" as they were called. It would show the landlords agents and his henchmen manhandling people out of their way whilst they ransacked the cottages and set fire to the roof thatch. That was how tumblings as they were known were handled. People old and young were rooted out of their homes, in the midst of chores and in the clothes they stood up in, with as much care as one would use handling a louse ridden wild dog. The agent's men would climb on to the thatched roof and fork the covering on to the ground. Often it was easier to torch the thatch and smoke out the sick and infirm or sleeping children in their makeshift beds. Their anguished cries fell on deaf ears. Very often they were trapped in their beds whilst the burning roof fell in on top of them. In some cases the discovery of the corpses of whole families was not unusual. Very often their corpses were found under a covering of straw lying on mud floors where they had been dead for some time and already been attacked by vermin (rats). In cases like this the houses were tumbled round the corpses making the homes their grave. Also it would show the anguish of relatives being parted; either to go to the workhouse or the younger ones to brave the dreadful conditions of the coffin ships to Canada or America, should they be lucky enough to gather up enough money to provide the cost of the passage. Large groups gathering at the little town to seek food and shelter where none was to be found and next, going to Fr. Patrick O'Malley the parish priest, asking him to go with them to beseech the landlord for his help. They would start out on that fateful dawn with the priest saying mass. In his sermon he would give advice relating to the journey and its purpose. Lastly he would give them his blessing and share what bread he could find, with mothers, to at least feed the little ones. Being pained to see a few of the grownups snatch the bread away and wolf it down. The curse of the famine!

During the return trek across the hills Fr. O'Malley's faith is not only sorely tried and tested but he questions it for the first time since he became a priest. The trek across the hills is merely a window on part of the journey but will hopefully give an insight in to the sufferings of the people who really made that journey and also the mentality of their oppressors.

Following the tragedy in a community, whose philosophy was as it is today, cut one of us and we all bleed, there would undoubtedly have been planned reprisals towards the landlord and his agent. The remaining inhabitants of the little town would not just be bleeding; reeling in the aftermath they would be haemorrhaging. Father O'Malley would have quelled the planned attacks; advising his flock to leave justice to a higher power. In his own way he would desire the justice as much as any man in his parish. Therefore, from the alter he would say, "and most of us, God willing, will live to see the sad, tormented demise of the perpetrators of the tragedy inflicted on the poor souls who perished in the hills." Then the healing would begin.

The Trek Across The Hills

Tenderly he laid her skeletal body on the snow-covered ground and gently closed her eyelids over the staring eyes that would haunt him for years to come. He removed his overcoat that he had wrapped round her to try to keep her warm. Someone else would need that coat now. Looking back over the hillside he saw the mounds of the other bodies already covered in snow. Was it only this morning that they had set out from the little town filled with the hope that Mr. Willis, the landlord would surely help them? As he wiped the green saliva from her mouth his heart was sore. Like many others Mary O'Neill had the tell-tale marks of green around her mouth. She had eaten grass to try to survive.

Mr. Willis had finally sent his agent out from his comfortable home to get rid of them. After all they were only peasants and he wasn't going to let them interrupt his luncheon with his guests.

"Go home, do ye hear? Go home now, there is nothing here for ye,"
bellowed the agent as he cracked his whip on the side of his boot.
His lackeys standing by in case there was any trouble.

"For Gods' sake man," cried the priest. "These people are starving.
They've been walking since dawn. Have you no mercy?"

"Go now father afore there's trouble," said the agent menacingly.
The priest quelled the angry scenes that followed. The lackeys had
guns. He didn't want the hangings or bloodshed that would
undoubtedly follow, on his hands. These poor people had suffered
enough. His pleadings to see Willis for a few minutes at least fell on
deaf ears. These men were well fed and had no sympathy for anyone
in his group.

How their faith was tried then. Murmuring dejectedly they turned
around like a band of ghosts to walk the hills again; people without
hope.
How long had he carried Mary O'Neill? One mile: maybe two. With
all his heart he willed her to live. Somehow he believed that if she
had lived so would the rest of them that was left. It would have given

him the hope he needed to help them onwards. But now that hope was gone. She was dead and he hadn't even noticed when life had slipped away from her. The wind swirled round them in great gusts. As he bent to bless her his spectacles fell onto the snow. He groped in vain to find them.

"God Almighty what are we doing here?" he cried raising his clenched fists in the air and slowly falling to his knees. As the snow settled on him he shouted to God startling the last few survivors. Michael O'Brien looked on unable to believe what he was witnessing.

"Why are you doing this to us, God?" he yelled as he pulled his white collar from round his neck and flung it on the snow-covered ground. "That's it; I have finished with it. Do you hear God? I have finished with it. I'm no longer a priest. I have failed them."
Michael went to step forward to assist the priest but a hand on his arm restrained him.

"Leave him be," said an old woman. "He needs to shed his tears too."

"Enough! Enough," cried Father O'Malley as the tears ran down his face melting the snow that had settled on his cheeks. The hopelessness of their situation engulfed him. Up until now his faith in God was unshakeable.

"If only Mary hadn't died I could go on. But now I haven't the strength to go any farther God." He would die here in the snow with what was left of his people. He had believed God would find a way to help them. How many were there left now but a handful? Surely there must have been five or six hundred when they set out before dawn with him as their leader, their inspiration and now look; he had failed.

"God, where are you?" he called his hoarse voice resonating in a muffled echo around the hills. "Why are you letting this happen to us? GOD! GOD! Can't you hear me? Oh God, please hear me," he cried as he buried his face in his hands and sobbed. He rocked back and forth on his knees no longer caring who saw him.

"My faith is lost now I'm afraid. All these years I have served you and especially the last four years of this awful plague, this famine that has beset us. I have watched so many die and at times couldn't even bless them never mind give the poor souls the last rites. There were too many; what could I do? One man alone and so many deaths! It sickens my soul. Fever, pestilence and vermin attacking dying, starving families! I can see it all," he cried as he rocked back and forth on his knees. He shouted about Queen Victoria's visit to Ireland earlier in the year and how the best side was shown for her.

"Would that she could see this hillside now! Oh God," he cried. "Why? Why?" but no answer came back.

A gentle hand on his shoulder startled him. Michael O'Brien couldn't stand anymore.

"Come now father, don't take on so, if you give up what has the rest of us left? Come now Father Patrick, don't take on so," said the boy hoarsely, as he picked up the priests round collar. He shook the snow from it and put in the priests' pocket. He groped further in the snow and found the spectacles. Michael rubbed them on the front of his frayed jersey before placing them crookedly on the priest.

"Here, let me help you up Father."

"You're a good boy, Michael. Please forgive me. You're so right; sure it's not God that's done this; it's man to his fellow man. Those who have plenty won't help those that have not."

"I know. I know, but we must be goin Father. We haven't got many left now and we must try to get them home."

The priest heaved a great sigh and tried to regain his composure. Michael helped him to his feet. Stiffly he stood up and looked around him at the same time straightening his spectacles. The crows were circling the hills like vultures waiting to strip the corpses. The dusk was falling but somehow the reflection of the snow from the ground gave the hills an eerie brightness. He must get on. They had to cross the river again.

"How many will we lose this crossing Michael?" he asked.

"A lot Father, look at the state of them that's Three times that river had to be crossed. In the first crossing poor Mrs. Clancy fell, shortly after they'd left the house of Willis, her baby in her arms. Sure it was like a waxed doll with the hunger. It was swept along in the floods. Oh! The screams of her he would never forget as she plunged after her child. They were the first casualties. Most of them were so weak that in the panic that followed many more were lost. God Almighty, why had they set out on such a fool's errand? Willis was never any good anyway. He should have tried harder to stop them, but enough; he must try and get the last of them home.

As they set out on the remainder of their journey he started to sing softly, "Faith of our fathers holy faith, we will be true to you 'till death." The others, in their weakened voices, joined in creating a faint echo over the hills as the crows circled above the body of Mary O'Neill already covered in snow.

With renewed strength Father Pat quietly prayed. "I'm so sorry God. I'm so sorry; please take them. Look at the state of them, their bones sticking out through them like skeletons covered with skin. Sure there's nothing left for them to go back to now. Take them kindly, please, in to your heavenly home. Please spare me to get home to Kathleen."

"Someone has to tell Kathleen what's happened here, Michael. I have to make it home"

"Aye you're right Father. Young Sean is without a father now, he's back there somewhere in the snow and she's without a husband; and you're without a brother. You'll have to help her to bring up the boy, Father"

"Yes I will, M

Looking at him Michael had his doubts, big an all as he was.

Softly he prayed as he trudged on through the snow with young Michael at his side. Already his steps were faltering. They surveyed the hill in front of them and beyond that there was another and then another.

"Please give me the strength to get home," he prayed, his tall frame bowed against the snow and the wind.

"Where are they?" Kathleen murmured to herself as she looked at the clock "They should be home by now."

She drifted off to sleep only to be awakened by a dog barking. She ran out of the little house by the church and looked down the hill. In the gloom of dawn she could see a lone figure stumbling through the snow. Barefooted she ran towards him, the hem of her skirts soaking up the snow. His steps faltered as he tried to run the last few steps she was shocked by his appearance; no round collar or overcoat on him. He looked as though he had aged twenty years since dawn. As she neared him he stumbled to his knees his outstretched hands reaching towards her. Their fingers touched. She tried to grab his wrists, to prevent him from falling, but they were wet from the snow and he slipped from her grasp.

"They're all gone Kathleen, they're all gone." His voice was little more than a hoarse whisper as he stumbled. "They're all gone," he whispered again and collapsed in the snow from exhaustion.

"Oh my God father in heaven," she cried. "He's dead."
Tears streaming down her face, Kathleen turned and ran back to the little church. She grabbed the bell rope and pulled on it. Harder and harder she pulled on the rope. Louder and louder the bell pealed echoing round the near desolate little town. A few people came from nearby houses. Kathleen pointed to the figure lying in the snow. The dog still barked. Kathleen, standing with her back to the

little church wall, still rang the bell staring with unseeing eyes out into the grey dawn. She didn't even see Father Patrick being carried in to the house. Tears streaming down her face she continued to ring the bell, clinging to the rope as it were a lifeline; how long she stood there nobody knows. As the cold overtook her, slowly she slid to the ground; the rope caught under her ample left breast and the bell at half knell: a death knell. There she died, with her tears frozen on her cheeks, leaving young Sean an orphan.

Father Patrick coughed. A hot drink was put to his lips. Someone was trying to rub warmth back in to his limbs. Slowly he recovered. Shivering violently he was put to his bed.

"Where's Kathleen?" he asked.

"She's still outside Father. God! We forgot all about her; the cratur will be frozen with the cold. We'll go and get her now, Father. She'll be in shock God love her."

Kathleen's frozen body was found in the snow with the rope bell still tucked under her left breast. Young Sean was asleep in his bed blissfully unaware of the tragedy that had taken place.

"Oh my God, she's dead the cratur, how're we goin to tell himself inside'n the bed? How are we going to tell the child? The Lord have mercy on her soul," said Bridie Connors. She made the sign of the cross and looked at her husband John, who took off his cap and did the same.

"Sure he's just another orphan now Bridie, another victim of this awful cursed famine. But sure he'll be one of the lucky ones; he's not goin to have to roam the roads foraging for food and shelter like most of the others that are left now after this night. Don't ye know Himself inside'n the house will bring him up? There'll be no workhouse for that lad thanks be to God."

"Thanks be to God, no," said Bridie nodding in agreement.

"Aye, you're right John; Father Patrick'll bring him up alright. We'd better go in and tell him poor Kathleen is gone too. It'll be the shock that killed her."

"We'd better tell him he'll have to take care of the boy too, Bridie!"

And so he did. It was from young Sean's lineage that the present day Fr. Pat O'Malley descended!

Story

The story opens at the farewell party for Father Pat O'Malley who has been a priest in the Bronx in New York for the past twenty years. His parishioners are mainly Irish, Black and Hispanic. He would ride his motorbike round the neighbourhood and he worked relentlessly with the youth trying to keep them off the streets and away from crime; out of reach of the law and in particular one cop called Greg Whyte. To him most of Father O'Malley's kids were "no hopers." But the priest did manage to keep most of them out of trouble by introducing them to music, sport, boxing and amateur dramatics. It took a while to get the youngsters to accept the amateur dramatics but in time and by linking it to the music the priest succeeded. The priest always carried an old black and gold tin whistle in his pocket and much to the delight of the boys would often play it to them. Leroy Brown called it, "The Black and The Gold," he thought that was cool. Leroy was one of the most troublesome children. He was a black kid 13 years old, and always in and out of trouble causing much heartache to his widowed mother, Matilda or Tilda as she was known. Just as Father Pat felt he had got through to the boy he received a letter from the Bishop advising him that he was being sent back to his hometown in County Mayo, as parish priest. True, this was his dream but now that it had happened he had mixed feelings about leaving. In truth he had grown to love the place and his people but realised that there never would be a right time to leave.

At his farewell party Father O'Malley was surprised to see Greg Whyte pushing his way towards him through the crowded room. Over the years a reluctant friendship had grown between the two men. Recently it had eased considerably when Greg called the priest to come to collect Leroy from the station. Somewhat surprised Father O'Malley headed for the station on his motorbike to find Greg and Leroy waiting for him on the pavement. The cop had resigned himself to the fact that the priest, who had the "gift of the gab" as he used to say to him, would only spring Leroy by pledging his word that he would keep him on the straight and narrow. He might as well save himself the paperwork!

On parting they wished each other luck and much to Leroy's chagrin Greg promised Father O'Malley that he would keep his eye on him.

Next day, the 7th of March 1974, almost twenty years to the day that he arrived in New York, Father Pat set sail for Ireland. Upon his arrival the first few weeks were spent on house visits and familiarising himself with parish matters and of course visits to relatives, distant and otherwise. Sadly he didn't have any close family. His granny and his mother had passed away during his time in New York. There were more than a few raised eyebrows at the parish priest riding around on a brand new motorbike, a very big surprise present from his parishioners before he left New York especially when through a bit of subterfuge his old bike was removed and Leroy was accused of stealing it. It was a big lesson for the priest.

Sean Hegarty advised him that plans were in progress to commemorate the anniversary of the 125th famine walk. The event was set for the last Sunday in May. Sean also told him that an American was coming to represent the Choctaw people. Father Pat was intrigued, after all wasn't it his grand uncle, Father Patrick, that led the famine walk. The priest told Sean that he was more than happy to leave all the arrangements in his capable hands.

So it was on a beautiful Sunday morning, in the month of May, with the birds singing and beams of sunlight streaming in a myriad of colours through the stained glass windows that Father Pat said mass for the victims of the famine. He noticed a little bird flying in and out of the church. It captured his attention but he went on, his gaze wandering, as he intoned, "Faith," he said again, "is a wonderful thing. It can help us move mountains, ford streams, survive against all odds and because we are all only human we can lose it and, only, if we are lucky enough find it again making us much stronger. Then, and only then our faith in God would be renewed in a much stronger way like that of my great grand uncle, Father Patrick Joseph O'Malley, whom I was named after, when he laid the body of Mary

O'Neill on the snow covered hill on that bleak mid-Winter night in the year 1849; a year when our country was in its death throes from famine. That night, pushed beyond human endurance, he both lost and found his faith in God."

The little bird was back again. This time it perched on top of the large wooden cross, bearing the tortured figure of the crucified Jesus, which was hanging on the wall at the back of the altar. It hopped from the wooden cross on to the shoulder of Jesus and began to sing, the sweet sound echoing round the church. The priest smiled. It was good to be home again. He had missed such simple things as the innocence of a bird in flight and song. In the silence that followed and as he watched the bird and listened to its sweet song Father Pat was momentarily transported back to the Bronx in New York and the events that led up to his departure almost two months earlier.

He could see it all now. Sitting at the breakfast table just tucking in to his bacon and eggs when Meg, his housekeeper, placed the morning mail on the table beside him. Quickly glancing through the envelopes he noticed one stamped with the address of the Bishop's office.

"One here from the Bishop's office, Meg. Can I read it?" he asked Meg who did not approve of eating and reading.

"Sure Father. The Bishop's office; what you been up to?"

"Nothing Meg."

"Well open it and see what he wants. I hope he don't want to move you, Father."

"No! Meg? But then you wouldn't have to put up with me and my old motorbike roarin in and out all hours." Father Pat mimicked her mischievously.

With eager fingers he tore the envelope open. Quickly he scanned the contents of the single sheet of notepaper with the official stamp of the Bishop's residence. The letter slipped from his fingers on to his plate of bacon and eggs. He stared in to space, picking up the letter again he reread it through the fat stains from his breakfast plate. He was going home. Going home at last!

"Why Father? What's wrong with you? Is it bad news?" asked Meg who had been watching him intently.

"No, Meg; just surprising news. I'm going home."

"What you sayin Father? You is at home; this is you home, ain't it?"

"No Meg, I mean yes, but I'm going home to Ireland; to County Mayo. Back to where I came from. That's what the Bishops letter says."

"You get on that phone right now to that Bishop and tell him you is goin nowhere. Do you hear? You is goin nowhere. What about Leroy and all them others? Who is goin to help them when you is gone? That Greg Whyte'll have 'em all locked up in no time. Well I'll tell you, you is goin nowhere. Hmm! No hopers he calls them. No hopers indeed. Don't think I don't know. They is only young and they need a chance same as everyone else: you is the only one who give them that chance. There was nothin here for them, that's why they was always on the street until you got em dancing, Lord knows why dancing but dancing an boxin an singin an everythin else. Now look at them. We is proud of them boys and girls now. Well least ways most of the time. They is still a few that need a bit more schoolin yet."

"I know Meg. I'll talk to Leroy Brown. He's coming good you know and I'll have a word with Greg Whyte down at the precinct. He's not such a bad cop: like all the rest of us he is only doing his job."

"Hmph! Tell that to Tilda Brown. Since her husband was killed in 'Nam she's had to bring that boy up on her own. The other day she told me she just never wants to answer the door because she knows it'll be someone to tell her that her Leroy's in trouble again. She's at her end with that boy. "

"I know, Meg. I'll talk to Leroy and the other kids as well. Don't forget there will be a nice young priest coming to replace me. He will work with them too and I bet he'll look after them very well."

But Meg was not convinced. As she walked away from the table Father Pat saw her pick up the hem of her apron and wipe her eyes. He knew she was crying. He got up from the table and went to his room. Sitting on his bed he looked around the room that had been his home for so many years. Did he really want to leave? He espied the old black and gold tin whistle on the shelf above his bed. He reached out and picked it up, fondly examining it he slowly put it to his lips. Blowing through it a few times to get a tone and gingerly placing his long slim fingers over the holes he closed his eyes and started to play. Gently his fingers moved in rhythm with his breath and as the music flowed he was playing the tune of The Sally Gardens. Once more he is back in the kitchen of his home in Ireland with his mother and grandmother. They loved to hear him play. His mother would dance around the kitchen floor whilst his grandmother sat in the corner by the open fire smiling her toothless smile and her crotchet needle and wool in her hands. Her fingers flew over the wool of the blanket that flowed over her knees and on to the floor in time to the music. They were happy days; but now they were all gone. They had both died in the intervening years. He had never seen them since the day he said goodbye and left for America. His mother was so pretty and vibrant even then. That last day when he was ready to leave they both asked him to play one last tune before he left. With great difficulty he played The Sally Gardens but noticed that this time his mother didn't dance or his grandmother didn't crochet. It was a sad parting. Their eyes seemed fixed on the two suitcases by the door. At their request he continued to play for a little longer until reality hit him. It was time to go and things would never be the same again. As the music stopped an awkward silence descended the room.

He looked from one to the other. His grandmother was the first to break the silence.

"Come here astore," and reached out to him. He bent to kiss her.

"This is the last I'll see of you," she said as she stroked his handsome face.

"Go on Grannie, I'll be back before you know it," he said holding her to him and stroking her forehead.

"No, Pat I'll not be here then but you go on and remember; always do your best wherever you go."

"I will, Grannie; I will," said Father Pat hoarsely.

"Come now, Mother, enough of that nonsense; of course you'll see him again."

"No, Maureen I won't. My time is not far off," and she smiled her toothless smile.

Father Pat laid his hand on her forehead and kissed her cheek; turning he picked up the flute and placed it in his inside pocket.

"Come on Mam, or I'll miss my bus." He picked up his suitcases and his mother conveyed him down the garden path where with sore hearts they embraced and parted. She stood and watched him walk down the road to catch the bus. The road that eventually led to America! And now he was going back. That had always been his dream but now it was about to become reality, was it what he really wanted? The timing was wrong. He still had so much to do; so much left unfinished. Then he realised there never would be a good time. As he continued to play the memories crept in to haunt him; like the night his sleep was disturbed by the voice of his mother talking to the doctor. Quietly he crept downstairs to the kitchen only to be ushered back to bed again. He heard the doctor tell his mother to send for the priest. Next day he was told that his daddy had gone to heaven. That's when he got angry with God for taking his daddy. He hadn't done anything to God so why should he have taken his daddy? He became a troublesome child at school. As time went on he was in and out of all sorts of trouble. His mother and grandmother constantly worried about what was to become of him. It was on the day he saw them cry over something he had done that he decided to try and fill his father's shoes; he would become man of the house and help them. . It was also at that time the new parish priest, Father Michael Moloney, befriended him and introduced him to music and boxing. Father Michael gave him the black and gold tin whistle. He was his saviour. Not only did he give him his time but also he encouraged him in his studies. In short he gave him a purpose in life. Learning became a wonderful journey. When Father Michael talked about history it was like stepping back in to that time. Together they fought the battles of long ago, sailed the seas and transcended time. It was much the same with geography; like going on a magical voyage of discovery to many lands and countries. Father Michael taught him about different peoples, their cultures and religions and how important it was to respect them. It was the same with all subjects and because of Father Michael he slowly, over the years, found a purpose in life. Gradually the dawning of his vocation had awakened within him and eventually led him to New York. That's why he understood Leroy and all the other kids on the street. They were just angry inside because of what life had thrown to them. He knew he had made a difference by working with them. Should he go or should he stay? Suddenly, his thoughts had been interrupted by Meg's knocking on the bedroom door.

"Father, you playin that Gawd awful flute thing again. Now you stop that caus it sure gives me the willies so it does; good and proper. Now you stop it d'you hear. You got a lot to do afore you goes home to Ireland and sittin in there playin that flute thing is not goin to get it done; so you come on outa there."

He smiled at the memory of Meg; God Bless her, she knew what he was going through and she made the decision for him and of course Father Michael had a hand in it too, God rest his soul. On his deathbed he had asked the Bishop to give his parish to Father Pat O'Malley and the Bishop had agreed. He was brought back from his reverie by a loud cough that in turn disturbed the little bird. He watched it fly around the church before flying out the door and in to the sunshine.

After mass they would walk in the footsteps of those who perished in the winter of 1849 to where the landlord's house still stood some twelve miles away. However, today would have an air of celebration. The children would have balloons; there would be ice cream vans for refreshment along the way. Music would be played and hymns sung at the memorial stone and finally the Rosary recited. In his sermon Fr. Pat talked about the hardship the famine victims suffered, especially, those who died across the hills on that never to be forgotten fruitless journey. He finished mass by giving his blessing and said "now we'll sing Faith of Our Fathers in their memory and the memory of Father Patrick O'Malley who led them."

The lead in to the hymn was played solo on a tin whistle and then joined by the swell of the organ to accompany the choir. Momentarily it was as if time stood still; even the birds appeared to stop singing and listen. It was simply a beautiful tribute to all those who died so tragically. Greg Whyte sat in the church of Saint Peter and Saint Paul, a rosary entwined through his fingers, more through habit than anything else. He looked across to the side aisle; yes, she was there but then he knew she would be; her being a good sincere catholic girl. Up at the altar Father Pat O'Malley turned to face the congregation as he uttered the words… Credo in Unum Deum, Patrem omnipotentem, Factorem coeli et terrae, visibilium omnium et invisibilium. At that point the congregation stood up and joined him, the hum of their voices resonating around the church… Et in unum Dominum Jesum Christum… Today, Father Pat had reverted to the Latin Mass as a tribute to the hundreds who in their weakened and sick state had lost their lives on that futile journey in the winter of 1849. They had died on the return journey from Delphi where they had walked across the hills to seek food from the landlord of the big house; they had died in vain; their journey to the landlord's house had been in vain. Greg noticed the black lace mantilla slip from Kathleen McCarthy's head. Quickly she recovered it and carefully placed it on her head again, covering her beautiful long wavy red hair. He caught her eye then; a smile briefly crossed her lips as she quickly cast her vivid blue eyes down to her prayer book. He continued to gaze at her. She was one of the most naturally

40

beautiful women he had ever seen. Quickly she stole another glance at him; beside him Leroy coughed gaining his attention.

"I think she likes you," Leroy whispered, giving him a knowing smile.

"Shh. Remember where you are, Leroy. Do you want Father Pat to see us now and spoil the surprise?"

Leroy shook his head.

"No Greg," he whispered.

Behind them a woman coughed impatiently. Greg raised his eyebrows at Leroy who dropped his eyes and lowered his head. Greg smiled to himself. He was secretly pleased that Leroy thought that Kathleen liked him because over the past few days he was aware of feelings stirring within himself that he thought were dead and gone, forever. But this was foolish. He couldn't fall in love now. It was not the time or the place. This was Ireland and he lived in New York and was only here at the behest of his brother to represent the Choctaw people at today's hunger walk. Kathleen was the local schoolteacher, and by what he gathered from Sean Hegarty, she was firmly ensconced here; had never been outside Ireland. He was a New York cop and today he could only guess at Father Pat's reaction when he discovered that not only was he a Choctaw but that he was here with his most troublesome "no hoper" Leroy Brown. Father Pat would surely think he had gone soft and probably think it was all to the good.

Imagine his surprise when, Father Pat, standing at the church door as the congregation walked out into the sunshine and Greg Whyte said "Hello Father. So we meet again."

"Greg, what in God's name are you doing here?"

"I'm here for your walk and I'm not alone," smiled Greg as he shook the hand of a very bemused Father Pat.

"You're not."

"Hi Father! How did I do on the Black and Gold?"

"That was you, Leroy?"

"Sure was Father."

"Well, I never?" Father Pat was speechless.

"What's your story Greg? Why are you here? How did you know I was here?"

"Well Father, that's a bit of a long story. But really I'm here to represent the Choctaw people."

"What? You a Choctaw, Greg! But you're a New York cop."

"I know Father. But I'm Still a Choctaw. We don't all live on the reservation you know."

"Well Greg, I don't know what to say. But it's great to see you again and this scallywag too," Father Pat beamed as he ruffled Leroy's hair.

"My brother is the Choctaw chief. Right now he is a sick man; because I live in New York he thought I was already almost half way here so he asked me to take his place and represent our people today."

"I'll tell you what; why don't the two of you come to dinner tonight because we'll have to get going now and then we'll have all the time in the world to talk? God but it's great to see you both; you're a sight for sore eyes!"

"Sure Father, I'd love to come but Leroy here has a prior engagement at the Kelly's home tonight. You see we've been here a few days and the young scallywag has been making friends already. Martin wants him to spend the night."

"But, I had no idea Greg. I knew from Sean Hegarty that an American was coming, but that's all."

"You weren't meant to, Father. It was all part of the plan, especially the Black and Gold for Leroy. We couldn't spoil his surprise for you. Could we? Sean arranged everything once I explained the situation to him."

"He did?"

"Sure. He was just as excited as we were. He just couldn't get over what a small world it was after all."

"Well, he's right. It is a small world. Who would have thought we'd be here together on an important day like today?"

"Who indeed, Father?"

Again Father Pat was speechless. He just shook his head and smiled.

"You a Choctaw; a descendant of The Trails of Tears and me a descendant of the priest who led the original famine walk!" With an arm round each of their shoulders he led them to the waiting crowd.

During the walk the priest and Greg had very little opportunity to talk. Greg was taken care of by the beautiful redheaded Kathleen McCarthy. During the walk he learned a lot about her. She was the local schoolteacher and lived with her father. He found himself being very attracted to everything about this girl. He had never met anyone quite like her in his life. They laughed easily together and seemed to have so much in common. He discovered that she had a very dry, mischievous sense of humour. Every so often Father Pat fell into step with them. Greg noticed the look of admiration in Kathleen as she looked at Father Pat. He wondered if Kathleen carried a torch for him after all these years. Perhaps that was why she never married. Kathleen told him a lot about the area and pointed out some of the mountains over which the people of the famine walk would have trudged. He found himself been drawn into something here but he was not sure what. Father Pat asked Kathleen to join him and Greg for dinner. She hesitated momentarily and then declined. The hesitation wasn't lost on Greg.

It was much later sitting by the fireside that they really talked. Greg noticed the silvered framed faded photograph of a priest next to which was a pair of very old spectacles on the pedestal table where his drink rested. He asked if this was Father Patrick Joseph O'Malley. It was then Father Pat told him the story of how Father Patrick led his people on the Trek across the Hills. (Flashback here to The Trek across the Hills.) Greg interjected every so often with similarities in the story of the Choctaw's Trails of Tears. (Further flashbacks.)

Many things were discussed that night and a bond of friendship was born that would last for the rest of their lives. They regretted that they never sat down to talk years before but being on opposite sides so to speak the opportunity never really arose. They marvelled at how they had met again. Greg and Leroy stayed with Father Pat for a few weeks. Another motorbike was secured and they happily agreed to let Father Pat be their guide and show them around. Greg managed to get some time alone with Kathleen and found he was falling hopelessly in love. He felt she was guarded with her emotions but at times he would have sworn that she was feeling the same towards him.

One day Father Pat showed Greg and Leroy two cottages on opposite sides of the estuary leading to a beautiful little harbour on their way to the beach. The beach Greg had already discovered. It was where Kathleen was often to be found walking when she needed solitude Sean Hegarty had told him. Leroy must see the Atlantic; The Bowl of Sand Filled with Tears! Father Pat tells them a story about the men who own the cottages. Each day when they tended their gardens their wives would bring out lunch at noon. The men would sit and whilst having lunch could chat to one another. The water acted as a conductor of sound so they never had to shout to hear. Leroy is intrigued by this and wants to try it out. Greg takes him on his motorbike over the bridge at the falls and along the road to the other cottage across the estuary. They have a conversation and it works.

"Smart ass priest," said Leroy to Greg.

"I heard that Leroy." The next sound to be carried over the water, from both sides, was hearty laughter.

Coming to Ireland opened up a whole new world for Leroy. For the first time in his life he was treated with real respect and without prejudice. He loved being at the Kelly's house. The first night he visited Martins home his little sister Mary was shy of him but intrigued because at the age of four she had never seen a black person. Slowly she edged nearer to where he was sitting and gradually overcame her shyness. When she thought no one was looking she wet her fingers in her mouth and rubbed at Leroy's hand. Then she looked at her fingers, the black hadn't rubbed off. She was puzzled and repeated the same thing again. When Leroy stayed black and her fingers stayed clean she just turned around and asked him if he wanted to see her doll. She accepted that Leroy was a new person in their home and that she liked him especially when he said that he would like to see her doll. Mary told him all about the doll. It was called Lucy and Santy (Santa Claus) brought it to her. From that time onwards she trailed Leroy. She had difficulty pronouncing his name and it sounded like Lewoy when she used it.

He loved the farm; riding on the tractor, feeding the animals, but was a bit scared of the sow; he thought her litter of seven piglets was cool. One night he was allowed to stay up and help watch a sick cow about to calf. The long wait was rewarded with the birth of a beautiful Friesian heifer (black and white) that was named Leroy in his honour. As time went on Mrs. Kelly allowed him to help her make soda bread, fruit loaf, scones and big Irish pancakes. All these he loved to eat especially when they were hot with melting butter dripping from them.

Martin's father showed him the new potato stalks growing in the garden near the house. He explained to him how the crop had failed in the years between 1845 and 1849 and how so many people had died from hunger and why, because the system with the landlords, the deaths and the immigration whilst at the same time all the food that left Ireland every week for England. He explained about the fungus and how it was carried in the wind and that's what blighted the potato crop. Leroy, whose days were filled with new things to learn and explore, had many questions for Mr. Kelly. He answered them all with patience and understanding. He impressed upon the boy how important a good education was. Leroy ached for a father of his own, one just like Martin's father. Suddenly he missed his mother but never missed things like burgers, coke and such like. Mrs. Kelly said he must bring his mother when he came back again. He liked it, when before bedtime; the whole family knelt around the fireside to recite the Rosary. Yes, Leroy was changing every day!

One day Father Pat and Greg borrowed a couple of trail bikes and followed the trail across the hills, the same trail taken by the victims of the famine walk. It was a beautiful sunny day. They stopped by the lake near what was the landlord's house. It looked beautiful nestling in the trees and today that beauty was reflected in the lake, as was the surrounding hills and the Sheffrey Mountains. They left the road and rode up over the ridge across the hillsides. High up and overlooking the lake they rested the bikes and just sat looking at the sheer beauty that surrounded them and yet wondering how in another season it could be such a bleak, barren and most desolate place. A place of death!

"It's so peaceful here, Father," said Greg, "How could a place of such profound beauty still hold so much sadness? The sadness still lingers, even on a lovely warm day like today."

"I know what you mean, Greg. I feel it too. It's almost as if the ghosts of all those poor souls, who died here a hundred and twenty five years ago, are still walking these hills. Well, I suppose it is their graveyard, God rest their souls. But they have left their mark alright, the sadness is almost tangible."

A companionable silence followed. Both were lost to their own thoughts. Over the past weeks a deep bond of friendship had silently grown between these two men from such different backgrounds; a transformation almost like a spiritual rebirth was taking place. Father Pat's vocation took on a new and deeper meaning for him. Now he knew what a vocation really was. Greg had seen the change in Leroy: one of the worst "no hopers". His own attitude to life was changing. He no longer felt like the cynical cop. New York felt like it was a million miles away; another world. Since he'd been here he had thought about his ancestors a lot. He felt their spirit draw near to him. Perhaps there was something to this fate and destiny his brother was always talking about. Whatever it was it was getting to him.

"Our people were fine people. Real good people and to this day prejudice exists against the descendants of the great Indian tribes; almost as much as it did back when they lived on their lands before they were removed to the new lands they called the wilderness. I never wanted to be an Indian; full breed, half-breed or any of the names we were called as kids. I was ashamed of being a Choctaw. When I was old enough I left my people and came to New York to break away from the past. My past, my peoples' past. Coming here to Ireland is like a trick of fate."

"How do you mean Greg, a trick of fate?"

"The feeling is here in my heart," he said pounding his chest with his fist. "I feel my ancestors drawing near, even here in this hillside; especially here in this hillside almost like I was meant to come here. This is the first time I have represented my people. It is the first time I understood about the Trails of Tears. I felt they should have stayed and fought for the old lands and not given up. Now I see it differently. I see the sacrifices they made by sending their meagre savings to help your people. They had very little for themselves in those times. They were just trying to scratch an existence from the soil in order to survive."

"Well, that's good, Greg. Isn't it? It is good that you did come here and represent your people."

"Yes. It is still there. I am a Choctaw. I feel I've come home to myself, home to my soul. Now I can accept who I am for the first time in my life and I feel proud."

A wave of loneliness and homesickness swept over him. He jumped to his feet and ran to the edge of the hill. Standing there, pounding his chest with his fists he shouted into the stillness of the mountains and the valley below him, "I am…Choctaaaw! I am…Choctaaaw!

His voice echoed round the hills and came back to him. Raising his hands in the air in the manner of offering to his ancestors and with tears of emotion running down his face and again he shouted, "I…am Choctaw…and… I…am…free! I …amm...frreeeee!"

Lazily Father Pat lay on the warm grass resting on his elbow absently chewing a blade of grass studying Greg. He realised that Greg had fallen in love with Kathleen and if he was not mistaken she with him. Somehow that pleased and saddened him. He thought back to the years growing up together. She was like his shadow. When he told her that he was going to be a priest he remembered how she cried and shouted at him.

"God has enough priests without you; he doesn't need you: I do. I love you. Damn you," she had cried as she turned and ran; her long red hair flowing in the wind. His own heart had ached for her because he did love her but not in the same way that she loved him. And so he went on to be Father Pat O'Malley. The night before he had been ordained she had asked him once more to change his mind and marry her.

Softly Father Pat called to Greg, "Greg, the sun has just rolled behind a cloud. I think maybe it's your ancestors' way of saying they hear you, they know the rebel has found himself. The rebel has finally come home to his soul. Now he can be his own master. One of his own people again."

The day came when Greg and Leroy had to return to New York but not before the Kelly's gave Leroy a party. It was a lovely summer's evening and Martin was playing his accordion with Leroy accompanying him on The Black and the Gold. The strains of the music wafted through the open door. In the distance Greg asked Fr. Pat where the music was being played

"That'll be Martin and Leroy. In a little while Paddy (Martin's Father) will join them playing the spoons and as the evening unfolds many neighbours will come bringing with them fiddles, concertinas and at least one bodhran (a type of drum) and there will be a great gathering and a bit of dancing. It is what we call a ceilidh."

"Can we go over, Father?"

"I wouldn't let you miss it for the world, Greg. Now you'll see proper Irish hospitality, and I bet Kathleen will be there too," Father Pat smiled mischievously.

"You are in love with her; aren't you?"

"Yes, I am Father. I'm going to ask her to marry me. Maybe even tonight."

"Good. It is time you were both settled."

And so there was a great evening of music, dancing and feasting the likes of which Greg or Leroy had never seen or heard before. Mrs. Kelly even brought Greg on to the floor to teach him how to dance a set. He didn't do so badly for a beginner she told him. Kathleen stood watching them tapping her toe to the music and clapping her hands unaware of her father studying her. In that moment he knew he had lost her and that it was time for them to have a talk. Later he noticed her go out in to the night. Mrs. Kelly caught his eye and he blinked and looked away. She went over and placed a comforting arm around him. There was no need for words. Greg noticed Kathleen leave the room. He followed her outside. She was standing at the end of the house. As he approached he heard her sniff and noticed tears glistening in her eyes. Silently he enfolded her in his arms and let her cry. He stroked her face and kissed away her tears.

"Come on now, Kathleen, why are you crying; nothing can be that bad."

"I'm just being stupid," she said smiling through her tears.

"No, you're not. You know I love you. Kathleen will you marry me?"

"It's hopeless. How can I marry you? What would someone like you want with me? Look I've never left this place and there's my father and yes I love you and it's all so hopeless," and she started to cry again.

"It's not hopeless. As for someone like me wanting you that's funny because that's what I have told myself about you. Why would a girl like you want me; a New York cop. I haven't much to offer you; only myself and my love. Kathleen will you have me? Think about it. I'll wait for you for as long as you want me to but please think about it."

"Give me a little time, please Greg."

"That's my girl," he said as he kissed her tenderly. "Love will find a way. My people always believe that. You'll see."

She slipped from his arms.

"Three months from today," she said. "Give me three months and no contact in between."

"Aw! Kathleen, that's a lifetime. No contact. You can't mean that."

"I do Greg. No contact and if you haven't changed your mind you can write and tell me."

"If that's what you want; OK, then so be it."

"Goodnight Greg," and she turned and ran down the road towards her own home.

He stood there and watched her disappear in to the night and knew that three months it had to be.

The party went on till the early hours of the morning and was enjoyed by all. Next morning there were tearful goodbyes at Kelly's house. Mrs. Kelly packed a loaf of soda bread and a rich fruitcake, which Leroy had helped her to make the day before, to take home to his mother. Martin gave him a Hurley and Mary gave him her doll. He didn't want to take it because it was her favourite.

"She wants you to have it, Leroy," said Mrs. Kelly.

"But it's the most precious thing to her; I can't take it Mrs. Kelly."

"I know it is Leroy, but she wants you to have it. Take it Leroy."

Leroy gratefully took the doll. He bent down and kissed Mary. She giggled and rubbed her hand on her cheek. She whispered, "I'll miss you Lewoy." That's when tears sparkled on a few eyes. Mr. Kelly gave him money to buy a present for himself and his mother. "Buy her a nice Irish linen tablecloth, Leroy. You'll get one at the shop in the airport."

Leroy promised that he would and sadly parted from his friends with a promise that he would come back again next year.

"All set then Leroy? I see you've got a Hurley going home. Was that from Martin?" said father Pat looking at the Hurley strapped to the suitcase.

"Yes Father," Leroy grinned.

"You know father, when we left New York, Leroy told me he was going to be a priest, but by the time we got to Shannon he was going to be a cop. Now he's not sure. Maybe he wants to be a farmer?"

"Oh no, I've made up my mind. I want to be a priest again."

"How come, Leroy?"

"Oh! That's an easy one. I'll have more time for hurling if I'm a priest."

"Is that so, you scallywag?" said Father Pat ruffling his hair.

They all roared with laughter.

"Best I send you to college then, Leroy my boy," said Greg as he looked anxiously up the road.

"She's not coming Greg. I spoke to her this morning. I know about the three months and I know Kathleen; she means it."

"Yes Father, I know, you're right."

"What's this Greg, Father?" Leroy asked puzzled. "You in love with Kathleen, Greg?"

"Yes Leroy and I've asked her to marry me but she said I have to wait three months before she'll give me her answer."

"Well that's good. She'll marry you then."

"How come?"

"Aw, you don't know anything about women; she didn't say no so that means yes."

They all laughed then and father Pat said, "I think he might be right."

And he was. Three months later Kathleen was anxiously waiting for a letter from Greg. It never came. On the appointed day she so was upset; the postman had been and no letter. She argued with herself for making him wait three months. She had missed him so much she couldn't stand it anymore. Her father had told her to go to him but she was too proud. She grabbed her coat and headed for the beach. She walked up and down the white sands listening to the sound of the surf for hours. Eventually she found a sheltered spot from the wind blowing in from the Atlantic. She sat huddled in the dune and let the tears flow. A hand on her shoulder startled her; she looked up. It was him. He knew where she would be. She jumped up and fell in to his arms. He knew his answer. Leroy was right when he told him not to write.

"She'll think you have changed your mind and she'll be beside herself. Just turn up and she'll fall into your arms."

And she did.

The End

The continuation to follow later;

It is intended that a sequel to The Forgotten People could follow entitled **Oceans Apart.** In the 1990's a group of people from Ireland went to Oklahoma to visit the Choctaw nation and together a large group walked the 500 miles Trails of Tears retracing the footsteps of the Native American Indians. They raised a lot of money along the way to aid world famine relief.

In my story Leroy will now be a priest in New York. Father Patrick Joseph O'Malley is still a parish priest back in Co. Mayo. Greg White, having found himself, as well as falling in love with and having married Kathleen McCarthy, has returned to work with the Choctaw people. They will all meet up again for The Trail of Tears walk, when through Greg's eyes, the horrors of that journey in 1831 will be told in all its sorrow and heartbreak. The story will have a happy ending! Peace reigns!

About The Author;

Vera grew up in the West of Ireland and moved to London as a teenager where eventually she married and raised a family. In her working life she had many jobs of differing persuasions but the greater part being in banking and Insurance. It was always her ambition to become a writer but a busy family life meant there never seemed to be enough time. Vera who is now retired lives in Hertfordshire where she intends to make writing a full time occupation. She has three children and seven grandchildren and is happily divorced...

Printed in Great Britain
by Amazon

45097251R00037